SO-EAU-300

Images: Sights and Insights

by

Mary K. Himens, SSCM

Photography by
Carolyn W. Treadway

Carolyn W. Treadway

Golden Apple Press
Champaign, Illinois

Printed by
Golden Apple Press Publications
313 N. Mattis Avenue, Suite 113-A
Champaign, Il 61821

Copyright 1996 by Sr. Mary K. Himens, SSCM. Illustrations copyright 1996 by Carolyn W. Treadway. No portion of this work may be reproduced without permission of the author or illustrator respectively.

ISBN 1-889463-20-5

ACKNOWLEDGMENTS

Images: Sights and Insights has had a long gestation period. Many forces, courses, readings and conversations have shaped the concepts and the metaphors found herein. Years of spiritual direction, retreats, contemplative living, active ministry, and being profoundly cognizant of my own human-ness and journeying have provided the content for the work. But I credit the photography of my collaborator, Carolyn W. Treadway, with springing me free from the many years of what I have called my "poetic dark night." For this, I thank her.

I also owe many thanks to my religious community, the Servants of the Holy Heart of Mary, especially Sr. Kathleen Mulchay, former student and present Provincial Superior, who has encouraged my pursuit of a Doctor of Ministry degree from the Graduate Theological Foundation in Donaldson, Indiana.

My natural family, and an incredible retinue of friends, former students and clients deserve gratitude for challenge, interest, and support. Thanks too, are due to my publisher, Dianne Henderson, who midwifed the project into present reality.

Lastly, I thank three priests who have shaped my spirit and soul: Rev. Anthony May, SVD, who led me as a child to a life in the Spirit; Rev. James E. Friel, who taught me love by sharing his loving ways of ministering; and Rev. Walter J. Burghardt, SJ, master homilist, and dear friend, who so generously penned the Foreword.

Thank you all,

Sr. Mary K. Himens, SSCM

PHOTOGRAPHER'S STATEMENT AND ACKNOWLEDGMENTS

Photography speaks its own language, a powerful, evocative language beyond words. Bypassing the logical brain, it touches the deeper, intuitive senses, and "breaks open" the viewer at many levels, unlocking what is already present in body, mind, heart, and soul. Visual images call forth one's own wealth of experience and memory, deepen awareness, and yield insight. All images in this book are intended to invite the viewer into her/his own creative namings, experiences of healing, and spiritual growth.

Photographs capture a split moment in time and space, which then reveals itself more and more fully as the image is viewed again and again. Through gallery shows of my photography, I have learned to see far more into my own images than I ever could have imagined as I looked through the lens to take the picture. I learned to see that which was already present even if I had previously been unable to see it. Through interactive dialogue with my viewers, I have begun to understand the unfolding of the photo image as a doorway to, and also as a process similar to, the unfolding of the Presence of God.

My life and spiritual path have been very different from that of a sister in a Catholic order. Far from being contemplative, I have had the incessant demands and rich rewards of a full family life with two professional parents and three very active children. My spiritual path has been filled with longing, frustration, and even "dark night" as I sought to find connection with God and spiritual community which could "speak to my condition." Yet, in the words of Thomas Kelly in *Testament of Devotion*, "over the margins of life...strained by the very mad pace of our daily outer burdens...and inward uncertainties...came a faint call...of richer living...from a divine Center." This call was very faint for me but also very powerful, so powerful it would never let me go. Photography has provided openings for me to hear and respond to this call more clearly. At first I used photographic books for centering as others might use scripture; later I went into God's world, with my camera and an open heart, to create my own.

Certain persons and places deserve special mention for their part in this creative process for me:

Mary Kay, whose doctoral project offered me the challenge of uniting my photographic images with her poetic ones in a collaborative process which helped me deepen and grow in clarity.

Roy, my husband, whose care and steadfast devotion have provided a bedrock for me and offered both of us the opportunity, diversity, and richness of sharing life for thirty years.

Our three adventurous, young adult, global-citizen children who inspire me in so many ways: Anna, whose determination, courage, and insight teach me much, and whose gracefulness touches my heart; Laura, whose integrity, strong beliefs, and artistry open my vision and my world; Nathan, whose wisdom, humor, and zest for life en-light-ens my own.

Elsie, my friend, who was instrumental in unlocking wonder, beauty, artistic expression, and spirit for me, and whose belief in me led to my first conceptions of myself as an artist.

Many precious friends who have companioned and sustained me on my path of life, creativity, and spirit, and many, many clients with whom I am privileged to go so deep.

Special places all over this planet, but most particularly Knollside, Lavalette, Grayrock, Sea Cairn, Evergreen, ParkLands, and the woods house on the Mackinaw, which have drawn me into the incredible beauty of the natural world, opened my heart, and enfolded me in Spirit.

Without these persons and places, these photographs would not, could not, have been taken. For the gifts of each and every one, I am profoundly grateful.

Carolyn Wilbur Treadway

*. . . she has no power
save the irresistible
force of love.*

FOREWORD

As primarily a preacher of the word, I revel in the kingdom of the imagination, the realm where the image holds sway. Scripture's lamb and cross and kingdom, shepherd and suffering servant; C. S. Lewis' *Tales of Narnia*, with unforgettable mythical characters like the lion Aslan, the unsafe, untamed Christ; Frederick Buechner's spider web, image of humanity - touch it at any point and you set the whole web a-tremble; Shakespeare's Falstaff, Benedick, and Shylock; today's popular symbols from country, pop, and rock to computer, car phone, and crack, from Madonna to Mother Teresa.

Where does Mary Himens, psychotherapist and spiritual director, fit into all this? She has taken a limited number of "core images," concrete realities "central to life and personality that help us connect with ourselves at some unknown, never-before-explored level." The realities are the stuff of every day: a path, a trailing wire, a stump, a pond, a morning mist, sculpted sand, arthritic hands. We see them in color and in black-and-white. Mary asks us to read them aloud, enter into them with all our senses, touch them to our own experience, name our own image/insight, speak of it to God or another we love, live the day in that new dwelling, in the power, the truth, of that fresh discovery.

Why? Not to while away the idle hour! To unlock my imprisoned self, to break open what is deep within me, to make whole (heal) what is fractured, to help me grow. To let the language of the right brain - imagery, metaphor, synthesis, relationship - transform me as the logic and reason of the left cannot; and to open us, first to ourselves, then, sooner or later, to God.

I find here an uncommonly rich experience of contemplation in Carmelite William McNamara's imaginative definition: a long loving look at the real.

Still, no explanation can substitute for the experience. So then, as we irreformable New Yorkers have traditionally urged, whether of lox and bagels or of the latest Vermeer exhibit, "Try it, you'll like it!"

Walter J. Burghardt, S.J.

Steps to Infinity

IMAGES: SIGHTS AND INSIGHTS

Dear God
Herewith a book do I inscribe and send
to Thee, Who art both its beginning and its end;
A volume odd
Bound in some brief allotted years,
and writ in blood and tears;
fragments of which Thou art the perfect whole
book of my soul.
Break Thou the sealing clod
and read me, God.

Sr. M. Madeleva, CSC, 1947

For all of my adult life, this poem has presented me with a central image: I am a book that is ever being written, its chaptered truth revealed in fragments by the vagaries of my life and being as I experience the "stuff" of life itself: growth, loss, love, relationship, failure, triumph, joy, and, above all, the Presence of God. Jean Dalby Clift, author of *Core Images of the Self*, would call this a "core image," something concrete which has been endowed with specific meaning, central to life and personality that helps us connect with ourselves at some unknown, never-before explored level.

The image may be rooted in an early memory: a poem, a story, a person, a song, a scene, a grief, a pain, a loss; or it may spring forth from an urgent quest for meaning, wholeness, healing, relationship, wisdom, unconditional love. The image-making mind, our imagination, bridges the concrete conscious experience and links it to the unconscious in a wonderfully mysterious way. It takes the observed, the felt, the known, the half-seen, half-known, and suddenly reveals more than one could have guessed was there. The imagination is as a nutcracker, cracking open the mind, the heart, the soul, to be "picked clean" of the hidden "meat," the essential mystery within. Hence, the concept which gives title to this work: IMAGES: SIGHTS AND INSIGHTS.

Imagery opens up to our yearning minds and hearts the whole of reality. Images, whether they be visual, poetic, symbolic, or archetypal, are filters through which we see everything as we yearn to grasp those understandings that are always just out of reach. In our quest to make sense out of our experience, to find meaning in our existence, to integrate the diverse aspects of our lives, the mind snags and toys with sights, sounds, emotions, events, "the known and the almost-known," drawing from them fragments of truth. These fragments help us connect at our deepest level, the soul level, with ourselves and with the Sacred. They shape our very being, or is it that they reveal that <u>word</u> of God that each one is---that mystery of "self" as it becomes more transparent to us?

Images are vehicles that crisscross the conscious and unconscious, carrying messages of truth, beauty, goodness, hope, fear, sadness, joy, even despair, from one to the other. Mercea Eliade named this bridging space "the inner landscape" when he wrote: "It is here, in the inner landscape where we can catch a glimpse of the Sacred. Symbols, myth, and images are treasures of the psyche and are the very substance of the Spiritual life."

This inner landscape allows us to gain a perspective from which we can see, somehow weigh, and know for their veracity all the incongruities, foibles, weaknesses, and strengths of human existence. This vision grants us insight into and beyond what we can immediately perceive, giving our vision both depth and a rich texture of meaning. Then, there emerges in the mind's eye, where we image forth and make the connecting leaps, something akin to Gerard Manley Hopkins' "inscape," that is, a seeing into, a clarity of perception we have never attained before. The photographer's captured moment, the composer's reflected sound, the dancer's slightest movement, the poet's well-hewn phrase - each contributes to this clarity of perception in its own way and with its own fragment of truth.

Metaphor contributes to this process immeasurably. As a figure of speech in which a word or phrase is applied to an object or action that it does not literally denote in order to imply a resemblance, metaphor challenges the imagination to find this resemblance or to create its own likeness investing it with its own symbolic value and meaning. In Aristotelian terms, the "metaphor consists in giving the thing a name that belongs to something else; the transference being either from genus to species or from species to species or on the grounds of analog." Most cultures affirm that in granting a name to some entity or person, power transfers, thereby empowering communication and fostering responsibility. Antoine de St. Exupery implies this same concept when, in *The Little Prince*, he has the fox tell the little prince that when you tame something or someone, you become responsible for it.

We can view the other classic figures of speech, simile, antithesis, and personification as types of metaphor. So, too, the extended metaphoric forms: parable, fable, allegory, myth, story. The metaphorical communication of these figures and types appeals literally to the conscious and symbolically to the unconscious. Therein rests the power of the image when introduced for therapeutic change and spiritual growth and development. The insight-bearing image, or metaphor, grants unbounded access to knowledge and wisdom. The archetypal Seer's vision, the Sage's truth, the Lover's ecstasy, the Celtic mystic's "thin place" are sacred sites opening into the spirit world, a world of unity, of integration, of freedom, and of grace where God's life and love are shared reciprocally.

Once we have accessed this inner knowledge and wisdom even to the slightest degree, all our aspirations and loyalties are transmuted and transformed. This re-orientation of seeing now what we have never before glimpsed serves as a reference point shaping values, ordering lifestyles and institutions, illuminating the unseen world. The mind, heart, psyche, and soul recognize the sacred and sublime in the familiar, be it in a flower, a bird in flight, a spume-kissed rock, a boiling pot, an empty horizon, or the inner ache of grief, loss, disappointment, or failure. The power-filled images juxtapose realities, force paradigm shifts, and introduce metanoic change as they offer new choices, new ways of looking at things, and tap into our experiences, beliefs, and ideas that may have been dormant in the mind.

Recent hemispheric brain research reveals the reason that the image-making faculties have such transformative power: imagery, metaphor, synthesis, and contextual relationship form the language of the right brain. Logical understanding and rational explanation are left brain activities that do not of themselves help us to feel or behave differently. For real change, - for growth, development, and integration, - imagery and metaphor are essential if not imperative. In psychotherapy and in spiritual growth work, figurative language, guided imagery, photographs, choreography, sculpting, anecdotes and stories, various objects and objects d'art all have a place and an important role. Naming the archetypes as they emerge and influence our lives, attitudes, and behaviors can prove very liberating.

As a seasoned pastoral psychotherapist and spiritual director, I have and do use these metaphoric modes to unlock minds, and hearts and souls, to break open the deepest truths and hungers of the person with whom I am engaged, thus initiating the process of healing. Several years ago I sought out the etymology of the word "healing." The same root gives us heal, whole, hale, and perhaps even hearty. Some scholars trace the word's origin to the Old English HYEL, with related meanings to bridging earth and sky. Others go back even further into the ancient Semitic languages and find it meaning "in God," or "inward dwelling of God."

The healing work of therapist and spiritual guide is always "inner work," a work of opening the creative centers through sights and insights, through restoring the contemplative dimension of the human person, so often lost, crushed out by a troubling childhood, and of which all are capable if taught to value and recapture that gift by way of mindfulness and practice.

I offer these photos and the accompanying poetic reflections as a stimulus to the peruser's own creativity in the hope that the mystic language of image and metaphor will offer healing. Many of the metaphors have long since been tried with clients, or have nudged the author on her journey to an ever deeper interior life. The photographer also has her own life-quest story to tell in her own medium.

That readers might find themselves "hale and hearty" and inwardly dwelling in God, may I recommend:

1. Read the reflections aloud slowly.

2. Enter into the photographs with all the senses: See color, shape and form; hear the sounds or the silence; taste and smell the salty air, the fresh water, touch the rough rock, the delicate bloom, or catch the mist.

3. Reread the text, reflecting on your own experience. What <u>word</u> is heard in your heart? What <u>image</u> emerges to open to you a new truth?

4. Name your image, your feeling, your insight, your reality. What energy does this image and insight give to you?

5. Speak of your image to God, to someone you love, or write in your journal.

6. Live the day in the truth of your new-found dwelling place, your own "book of the soul", inscribed and read by God!

"Every creature is a book about God."
-- Meister Eckhart

Sr. Mary K. Himens, SSCM

Images: Sights and Insights

Contemplation

Beginnings

In crawling from the waters,
    (as once all life emerged
        from primal sea...
        "In the beginning...")
    the child claims earth and being
        as its own.

In that stark gaze, so struck
    with openness and trust,
        ALL possibility is bared;
        ALL potentiality is poised;
        ALL prospects held in promise...
    As "In the beginning..."
        Life ever beginning anew.

Doorways Into Doors

Can anyone pass a gaping doorway
     without pausing to peer within,
     the sight an open invitation
     to explore?

Inside are shreds of memory,
     and webs of waywardness;
     harsh words, and broken promises
     that split and break apart
     each fragile family tie.
This space is filled with ache
     and wounded human hearts.

To find perspective, accepting meaning...
     to know the truth that heals,
     demands a reaching out...
     requires the risk and courage
     of opening the inner door!

A Question of Change

"Was there always resistance to change?" I ask.

When first flint lighted tinder,
      and pierced round rock became a wheel;
When bark of birch was stretched to frame
      and launched upon the tide;
When arrow shaft was feather-fletched
      and sapling, sinew-strung, first bent into a bow;
When bird's fine bone became a needle
      and twisted hair a thread;
When mud was molded, shaped in squares
      and stacked to form a shelter's wall;
When bogs were drained and dressed
      and peat first cut as fuel for winter warmth;
When King's divine-right was vanquished
      and people claimed their power?

"Was there always such resistance?"

The listing could go on and on across
      the endless years, the eons, and millennia:
      Papyrus into paper; tin into a horn;
      Maps to prove the world was round;
      And instruments to chart the skies,
      Or peer into a heart;
      Horseless carriages; Wright Brothers' folly.
      X-rays, Cat-scans, MRI's; optic fibre thin;
      Cell-phones and stereos, T.V.'s interactive;
      Hubbell scopes, instant film, and micro-chips;
      Flights in space and walks upon the moon;
Each takes its' place in time
      and in the lives of all.

With such evidence before me,
      of resistance so perverse,
      Why should I find surprising
      my heart and will's reluctance ---
         the slow-paced change ---
         the snail-like metanoia,
         the creeping transformation
         into virtue out of selfishness and vice?

Gull-Like

So often this is how I am ---
        caught between the land and sea,
        hesitant to move, doubtful, and quizzical
        about which way, and how, and why.

So I stand fixed, as rooted in the now moment
        as if there were no past to give me reason,
        and no future to give me hope.

God lives in Eternal-Now-Ness.
        So I've been told, and do believe, I think!
Perhaps this perplexing moment, this "now"
        is some unfathomable gift,
        a "now" in which to share
        the "NOW" of His own "NOW-NESS" ?

The Yearning

Fields stripped ...
            for resting.

Doors opened ...
            for waiting.

Tree topped ...
            for nesting.

Wires stretched ...
            for listening.

ALL is in the yearning...
            yearning
                for the MORE.

Transforming Promise

Beautiful blossoms
    hold a bountiful promise
    of a bearing yet to come.

The harvest will be plentiful
    when bees and breeze
    have shared their pollenating skill.

And early summer rain has plumped
    the hard green rawness
    that an August sun will kiss
    to rosy sweet...

        A ripened promise!

Untutored Wings

The challenge of my being
        is to soar above the wastes
        that in me lie...

The chaos, the abyss,
        the yawning vastness of the utter <u>me</u>...

But to soar,
        to swoop, to dip,
        to hold one course, ---
        resting in a Pentecostal wind,
        the Spirit's breath,
        is yet beyond my ken.

Earthbound is the wing untutored in the NOW.

Solitary Journey

To walk alone
       in snow-drenched woods,
       with only stark outer bareness
       as witness to the void felt deep within,
       requires unfathomable trust,
       a well-tried faith, a firm conviction,
       that ultimately each of us treks
       a path no one has ever trod,
           - nor ever will.

Though many another may stand sentinel watch,
       may arch and bend protectively,
       as do these trees,
The way that opens to us
       is a solitary journey
       to our own center
       and to God!

Prayer of the Troubled Soul

As in hours at the birth of morn,
      or moments fleeting by the day,
Hushed, expectant, weight-some thoughts
      come to grip me and to stay.

To loosen, lose them, bid them gone,
      I pray; I strive, but am not able.
They cling, as any rider seed;
      they multiply, divide and breed,
      grow to stature, upon me feed,
As had some mighty chef prepared
      for them a gala festal table!

I know not why
      I troubled be
      by darkness, doubt, and loathsome fear.
But pray, "Dear God,
      some light to see
      beyond this fog, so dense, so drear."

Breakthrough

A late winter snow has come to cloak
with downy warmth the wintered
ground of being, hard frozen
by the frosty winds of fear,
of fate, of fury!

Strange, how it has gentled the edges,
softened the brittle bite of icy stream,
and freed a beauteous bounty
of bubbling life to flow.

What paradox!

The seeming cover births the breakthough!

Awakening

Sunlight crept through the opaque drapes ---
      so carefully constructed and hung protectively ---
"No surprise encounters, thank you!"
     Yet somehow light had stirred
        the sleeping one.

Covers snatched higher,
      pillow burrowing,
          turning on the other side,
            curling to a ball,
Nothing kept the beckoning rays away.
"No encounters wanted, thanks!"

Daring, risking, all out of the question.

    But then ---

Reluctantly exposing SELF
      to the relentless light
      come bursting into heart's room
      as some impatient lover,
The timorous soul, awakened
      to the moment's mystic grace, cried,

    "Yes! Oh yes! Oh yes!"

Creation's Dance

Morning mists wear veils,
      softening, chastening the brash display
      as autumn's haughty haridans
      flaunt their colors bold.

Morning mists play match-maker,
      daring the watery depths
      to kiss an ashen sky, and merge -
      becoming One --- Genesis re-told.

Creation's dance goes on!

Golden Path

I pondered long the contrast
    of golden leaves flung high above,
    and browning carpet on the path below...

    "How came it so?

Perhaps the child in my path-seeking, leaf-shuffling feet
    held close a wisdom my mind seemed not to know...

    "Paths are meant for following,
        no matter where they go,
    And contrasts share a mystery
        no matter what they show.

Stumps

Some days are "stump days."
    Thrusting trunk, cut abruptly,
        denuded of its greening canopy.
    Tangled roots, twisted loose from anchorhold
        then sanded bare by waves relentless,
        and hidden grain, and grit, and stone.
    The whole at last tossed up ashore
        for bleaching in the sun,
    Like lost days, somehow starkly beautiful,
        provocative, evocative,
            waiting, waiting...
Some lives are "stump lives."
    Dreams of youth sawed cleanly through, long since,
        by fate, or selfish whim.
    Roots of wholeness callously ignored,
        or shallowly planted in the surface
        of society's sad shore,
        truncated, bereft of nurture, challenge, hope,
    Lost lives... yet starkly beautiful,
        provocative, evocative,
           and waiting, always waiting...

For a human touch to give the gift of GRACE.

Spring Surprise

My fancy says that fairies
hung these florals
overnight
to shame the gray bark branches
into greening!

Each bud holds promise,
each bloom fulfills...
the whole, so delicately
bedecked with pregnant meaning!

Land of Falling Waters

NO falls are silent witnesses.
Instead, they spill tumultuously,
consuming the rocks below,
while sprays and foams and greening power
give LIFE.

How like human heartache!

At Play

Clouds play tic-tac-toe
    on cross-hatched contrails
    in the spring-blue sky.

That sky, tracked and scarred
    by jumbo jets ceaselessly streaming
    ethereal paths toward who knows
        which main street,
        what metropolis,
        which megalopolis, or
        what unknown village
        of some far hinterland.

The busy-ness of global life
    leaves leisure to the clouds alone;
Earth children, commerce wrapped,
    big deals in hand,
Forgetting play, have lost the game!

Like Daring Bird

A flash of wing into the gilding tree
Creates a gentle stir; the branches sway
As to a silent beat, - as dancers say,
And leaves drift down, flung spume on colored sea.
But look! A bird rides leaf toward earth, to be
Afloat, sure draft, --no fluttered wings at play.
Until near crashing-time, at risk to stay
It shakes and lifts its tiny body free.

Unrivaled boldness, never seen before.
So like our courted dangers, running risks.
Undaunted by the warnings timely given,
We blindly dash and rush to clasp the MORE,
Whatever captures fancy, -- baubles, disks, ---
All dross to which our flailing hearts are driven.

Purposeful Grace

What hidden purpose moves
     you on at such a hurried pace?
Is it something that you know,
     or see, which rests in the beyond,
     half-hidden, half-revealed by spume and foam?
Or is it that you seek serene security of sandy shore
     or choicest morsels newly cast thereon?

But even in your seeming haste
     there is an urgent grace. . .
     a playful, prideful, persistent presence,
     a leggy stretch toward pressing plan,
Empowered by depth of inward light and peace,
     moved onward by the hungered quest
     for the goodness and glory of God!

"The charity of Christ impells us. . ."

Questing

With eagerness I quest
        the object of desire.
No stone I leave in place
        no spot is passed untouched.
I search and scan each face;
I pierce, then scorn, each eye.
For nought in east or west
        is found with flame afire.

The quest without me ends. . .
        What use to wander hence?
No drink will satisfy,
        no food, this hunger stay.
"Oh, restless heart," I sigh,
"You know well where to search."
Desire, or passion, bends
        beneath the cry; in SILENCE.

Ruby Beach

The undertow of life
    pulls at me again
    and again and again.

Healing comes
    as tidal flow and wear,

Incessantly eroding,
    inexorably, but gently
    creating
    a new ME.

Quiet Pond

Murky waters mar the
　　mirrored glory
　　of red-crowned, gilded beauties
　　clinging to the water's edge.

But those already stripped,
　　or those submerged in part,
　　somehow rest serene in mirrored truth.

Now what does that say?
　　What echo can be heard?

"Unless a grain of wheat..."

Folded Inside

Sharp green brightness shatters sight -
        too much for the eye.
Sticky, prickly poppy buds
            nod assent to passing breeze
            and humbly bend with knowingness
Of what magnificence rests
            folded tightly in, -
Awaiting the stunning sunshine rays
            to burst them into
            unspeakable color.

Our truth is also folded in;
            our knowingness awaits
            the healing, freeing touch,
            the divinely human warmth of love.

Measure For Eternity

Time is a tyrant with broad sweeping hands,
Measures for moments in fast moving sands,
Placements for shadows on circular dials,
Small drops of water in little glass vials,
Rubies and diamonds set on a wrist,
Rhythmic rocking and pendulum's twist.

Man is ingenious in measuring time.
Yet rare is the thought of its import sublime.

The Ache

The hushed, the dread, expectancy has
          Frozen thought as chalice glimpsed.
The heart so dead...
Alone, one knows Gethsemane.

Strange heart,
so fickle in its trust...
so paralyzed by fear.

Homestead's Hide And Seek

Voices shaping love and laughter once echoed here;
        now only winter winds whistle
        through the paneless windows,
        sweeping across the warping floors
        remnants of past months' leafy fall...
        their dryness scratches,
        catches on the splintering wood, then
        as some long-ago playful child,
        skitters to hide in the corner.

One visits the decaying house,
        the sheds, the barns, the woods,
        hoping to capture sights and sounds...
        remnants of long-ago family folk...
        and find sustenance anew from roots
        plunged deep within this soil, these fields,
        once turned by plough, sweat-stained but
        steady, in ancestral hand.

It's cold, bleak; snow has fallen early
        or have I waited too long,
        too late in seeking,
        what now I know is hidden too well
        for the easy finding?

Dancing Reality

Lithe young ladies,
    poised to soar,
    firmly plant an un-shod foot
    To grounded stay.

Dancers three,
    stretching, reaching,
    meaning unseen sought...

        One looks toward what has been;
        One faces what is here;
        The third seeks what will be.
Past...
        Present...
                Future...
                    Form one reality!

Grief Has Ragged Edges

Grief has ragged edges. . .
      as cut-off jeans, torn and straggly,
      as shirt cuffs, worn and frayed,
      as collar fold-line thread-bare thin. . .
So are the jagged lacerations of the human heart
      which grief has claimed.

The paralyzing pain of loss,
      the melancholy misery of mourning,
Stretch out entangling tentacles of grief
      consuming fragile faith's perspective on eternity!

Progression in Folly

Unto folly had I sought:
      Kingdoms high, with right-hand places,
      Golden charms and sense's pleasures,
      Each containing earth's poor treasures.

Unto folly have I loved:
      Nought remains but shattered crystal,
      Slivered remnants, useless pieces,
      Nought survives when dreaming ceases.

Unto folly now I live:
      Lone, the worm, among earth's moss.
Unto folly now I love:
      Love, the folly of His cross.

Blue Mesa Legacy

Where once a river ran, breaking over boulders
    in joyful bubbling foam and froth,
    its westward current swift to conquer rock
    and carve a canyon dark and deep,
Now rests a placid lake refecting Colorado sky,
    with fishing boats dotting its crystal surface
    and trophy trout trailing on heavy lines.
Abundance and beauty grant delight!

But when the west wind warrior suddenly
    worries the waves to troughs,
Most fright-filled fisherfolk quickly
    abandon the bobbing craft
    to claim the safety of the rocky shore.

Life's little cataclysms and stormy turmoils
    distract and disturb the surface of my soul
    as do these waves, whipped to frenzy
    by prevailing westerlies.

But deep down, in well-worn channel bed,
    swift flows my life's strong current,
    resolutely carving yet another canyon. . .
    a place of union, and of peace.

Beyond the Veil

The masterful Director
      ordered scrim across the stage,
      "Hang it from the trees, if necessary."
      And so it came to be!

The light Technician,
      knowing well his business, said,
      "Back lighting'll do the trick."

And behold...
      colors shimmered from beyond the veil!

Untouched

The covered pot boiled furiously:
     broth foaming round the rim,
     spilling with abandon down the sides,
     leaving sodden detritus everywhere ---
          with everyone,
    No one left untouched.

Removal of the cover only made it worse:
     life's sad soup boiled on -
     - a witch's brew of haste,
          neglect, abuse, and loss,
     flinging wide remnants of each pained event,
     to cling on innocent and guilty --- all the same---

     No one left untouched.

Lowering the heat had some effect:
     but left un-sureness, no security
     that some stealthy hand would not,
          could not,
     turn it up again as had happened
          many times before.
     Fearful, alone, cut off --- untouched.

So the pot was put on "simmer":
     - a slow and bubbling boil -
     the lid was gently lifted,
     - slid to the side a bit -
     to let the steam escape.

The roiling, boiling contents could now be studied:
          - each nameless dread
          - each haunting memory
          - each aching grief and loss
          - each unappeased hunger
     in turn was named, and known, and healed.

The recipe had changed -
The life, now fresh and new, ---
          untouched, but touched, and touching!

Arising from the Wreck

Trailing wire yet captures
all that's left
of guardian fence,
Its laths, warped, cracked,
shattered, scattered
by hurricane brutality.

Yet somehow, I walked away,
- beaten, frail -
rising from the wreckage
of my life's well-used defenses
and felt FREE!

Virgin Territory

Waving prairie grasses,
      sun-kissed to taffy,
      finger-pulled by blustery breezes,
      stretched, horizon to horizon,
         awaken wonder. . .
Who first shouldered
      through the waist high
      seas of green or gold,
      spanning from sky to sky?
What secret journey's quest
      bade the seeker plunge on ahead
      into that endless vastness,
      mile after mile after mile?
Whence came the seeds,
      source of this abundance,
      so profligately cast
      into the rich black loam?
The wonder of the Who, the What, the Whence -
      and countless other questions,
      while the simple glory of the scene itself,
      draws one into mystery, mystic meaning,
         --- un-explored and un-expounded ---
         --- within, without ---
           virgin territory.

Who Knows. . .

The old tree had rotted from within,
    like the liver of an alcoholic.

Who knows what boring beak, -
    nut hatch, woodpecker, or tiny beetle -
Conveyed fatality and opened conduit
    for burrowing beasties to feast
On ring, after ring, of ageless growth?

Who knows what winter wind,
    or swift summer storm, sent
The worm-riddled trunk crashing to earth?
But there it lay,
    year after crumbling year,
Still feeding creatures small, - innumerable -
    generation after generation.

Yes, I remember stumbling over these remains,
    more than once in my wanderings,
Crushing the pulpy mass with heavy steps
    and cursing the sudden instability
    of seeming stable form.

Strange, today as I passed by, -
    this fragile beauty, -
    (called Indian Pipes, I'm told)
Arrested my steps
    and held my mind entranced.
How could such fragile beauty emerge
    from messy mass of death's decay?

Who knows the magical mystery?
The mystic delicacy of life from death?
That tentative balance, and stern economy?

Would that I understood these paschal happenings!

Leaning Into The Lord

Wintery wanderings
      were wanton escapes
      from doubt, distrust,
      discouragement profound.
Protective layers had been pierced,
      penetrated, defiled, and nullified.
The need to trust again was great,
      to feel secure and sheltered
      by another's solid strength.

Awareness came, as dense woods
      opened to a clearing.
For there, in a moment's sharpest clarity,
      the resting tree gave answer:
            "Try leaning into God!"

As If...

My eastward window invites the sun to enter
        and caress my room. . .
Sometimes it is just that. . .
        a caressing softness, a gentle glow to bask in. . .
           AS IF
        a LOVER shares this solitary space with me.

But then again,
        a piercing shaft cuts through,
        stabbing the carpet, wounding its dusky, earthy tones. . .
           AS IF
        to say, "Remember, thou art dust, and unto dust. . ."

Or yet again,
        a single ray selects a single volume
        from upon the crowded shelves,
        pointing a Divine finger. . .
           AS IF
        to say, "Read this, and only this!"

But today,
        I am suddenly aware of veils. . .
        for the sunlight dances, wearing wispy veils,
        trailing filmy shadows
        from wall to desk to bed to floor. . .
           AS IF. . AS IF. . .

        luring, enticing, seducing,
        whisking me away breathlessly
        into the very Heart of Being. . .

           Ah -   AS IF !

Lesson Profound

Devilish, dancing daisies
     with button-bright faces,
     mirroring the sun,
laughed as I told my loneliness.

To end their endless
     knowing nodding,
     with vengeful heels,
I stamped the clump to earth.

Midst twisted stems and battered leaves,
     their bruised faces,
     yet golden, more golden e'en,
bravely smiled heavenward.

Then --- only then ---
     Did I, the fool, understand!

Absurd Paradox

Joy / Pain
floods / parches
fertile fields / desert spaces
where songs burst / where sighs pierce
dikes of humanness / aches of loneliness
ecstatic stirrings / muted cries
vibrant Life / sacral DEATH

Death / Life
Pain / Joy
O sterile fruitfulness / and fruitful sterility
A loving loss / and losing love
Absurdity in order / and ordered absurdity.

"And Pippa passes. . ."

Joy-Less

It's weathered a bit, --- dulled,
      half-hidden in the dross of every-day-ness.
The word that sprang to life ---
      no longer heard ---
      drowned out by myriad clamorings.
The gift, so freely given -
      so rich in promise -
      set aside as not fulfilling,
      all it claimed to be.

Any wonder, then, the gift of joy
      resounds not in my soul?

Late Morning Mist

From hidden hermitage the scene is viewed.
    Still waters. . .
        Quiet mists. . .
           Muted mirrors. . .
             Tumbled,
                Blackened,
                   Barriers -

Is this the image of my SOUL?

Circle of Love

How does one tell of Love's new realms of love?
Wherein repose, yet action infinite
Is felt to BE, EXIST, the ALL in it,
The breathless act, as when a swooping dove
Flies free at last, or somersaulting child,
Head tucked with heels, turns over and over,
For the sheer joy in it. So love turns round
Until a circle full is formed. In love,
I pour myself before Him until there is no sense of ME,
Only to find myself anew, --- enriched in Him.

Little Sisters

No rivalry here to fracture loving bonds. . .
  only the protective arm of elder sister,
  holding safe the littler one,
  while clasping firm her blanket
   for security.

Grown now, each wends her way, becoming WOMAN,
  with changes, chances, mutations,
  failures, gambles and uncertainties,
  with lurking shadows,
   without,
    within.

May blanket, bond, and loving arm
  still safe security supply
  as course is set, and journeying begun.

Gathering Rainbows

When reassuring rainbows arch not
    across my doubt-dark sky,
I search God's world and create my own.

Summer makes it easy: Gardens yield
    geraniums red, lobelia blue,
    pansy faces violet and yellow bright,
    all rimmed around with greenest green.

October skies give up their azure hue
    to blend with maple's red and gold,
    and asters nod their royal purple heads
    against the pine's tall-towered evergreen.

At other seasons, shapely bottles
    hug the window pane and grasp
    the shreds of sunlight to produce
    faint prism-shaded rainbows
    on the counter, floor, and wall.

As do all the rainbows I have gathered,
    these bottles carry scents and secrets
    of their former lives and selves.

They hold my whispered hopes,
    my fast-held dreams and wishes,
    till rainbow promise be fulfilled.

God's Sentinels

These tall brave guardians
     withstand the changing seasons,
      faithfully fulfilling the work they have to do.
I've seen them lushly clothed in green,
     then bedecked with golden plumes.

Today, a starkness marks them,
     as with feet deep blanketed
     with snowy winter warmth,
They cast their shadows long,
     doubling their numbered strength
     against opposing forces,
     in black and white they stand. . .

God's Sentinels

The Gunny Sack

It was just an old potato sack
      of burlap, tattered and worn
      at the corners,
Slung over the shoulder for handy
      access to stuff
      his "treasures" in.

For years, he'd gathered bits and pieces ---
      brokenness, abandonment, and loss,
      lies, betrayals, and feelings long denied.

All had metamorphed to anger,
      an anger so profound,
      the heart was bitter.
And bile was spewed with every spoken word.

To air the putrid mess,
To expunge the rage within,
To keep from further stuffing,
Required an artful, gentle, patient use
      of scissors to cut open a corner,
      of scalpel to lay bare the wound,
      of forceps to excise the cynicism,
But, above all, an abundant application
      of the healing balm called LOVE.

Paradise

Paradise is a jewelry shop ---
      we are as thieves,
      stealing the gems!

Trickles of Grace

Arthritic hands cannot turn faucets tightly; -
        they drip, or run a trickling stream,
        wantonly, wastefully, profligately, -
        a flagrant challenge to a frugal steward's style.
The lesson, "Waste not; want not!"
        well-learned at Great Depression's door, -
        oft recalled across the years, -
        now echoes with discord in the ears.
The mind makes up excuses:
        "At least the pipes won't freeze!"
        "The water's always fresh and cool!"
        "The water bill CAN'T go up THAT much!"

But perhaps there is another rationale -
        a logic and a wisdom to be gleaned from faucet flow.
This weakening of hands, once strong,
        that long held tight the reins,
        directing all with prudent, parsimonious power,
Now gives respite, allowing inner soul and heart
        to be renewed, washed and bathed
        by drips and runs and trickles
        of life-giving grace.

Egypt's Path

A window shaped of fractured glass
      portrays a family in flight. . .
      Christianity's first refugees,
      escaping envy's sword and power's paranoia.

The Silent Night of birth, of shepherds' awe
      and angels' "Glory!"
      gave way to fear, to death, and
      Rachel's wail!

Today, across the centuries,
      others gather the shards of broken lives,
      lives shattered by arsenals amassed
      in cupidous quest of land and wealth and power.

Lord of the fleeing refugee,
      the hungry, the maimed, the lost,
      the voiceless and the massacred,
      Let not our eyes be blinded, our voices silenced,
      our quailing hearts hardened by
      scene after scene, after scene,
Of fractured glass, shattered lives,
      of stumbling feet, and children's cries.

      Egypt's path is OURS for it was YOURS!

Spring Sunset

Silvery down drifted aimlessly
    across the blue satin comforter sky
    coming to rest on edge of lazy day's couch.
Fleeting strands of fiery lady's
    gold-bright tresses tossed farewell kisses
    from earth's doorway toward the floating down
    which eagerly stretched to catch them,
    bursting into colorful delight!
Other impish wisps ran dance-like to capture
    the stray capricious symbols of the
    fading lady's love.

I sat alone, a speck on the rolling
    green plush that formed a hill.

THEN. . .
    A diamond chip quivered expectantly,
        warming to a promise as it captured
        the last blown kiss.

The evening star — spring day was gone.

Epiphany's Song

Gold - precious, pure and chaste
      cleansed by flaming fire's taste.
Incense - sweet perfume of prayer
      rising throne-ward, God is there.
Myrrh - pungent, bitter, suffering's coin,
      wear the smile and gird the loin.

Triple gift and triple vow
      offered in the Eternal now.

Replication

The darkened chapel held
      a golden ostensorium,
Radiant with Wheaten-Presence
Touched by flickering flame,
Drawing believer's vigil gaze
      into its central eye.
            "My Lord is here!"

But outside,
Outside in rain-fresh, chapel-valley-sky,
The Ever Profligate One ---
Against darkening mountains
      and hovering clouds, ---
Sets another Ostensorium,
      another EYE!
And with
      focussed shattering,
      bounded scattering,
      radiant light-full-ness
Wrenches from believer's throat
      the sigh of awe. . .
      the cry of ache. . .
            "Oh yes, My God is here!"

Redbuds in Blossom

Some call this the Judas Tree,
    for legend says it held
    that traitorous one
    who hung himself,
    despairing of his act.

I've never believed such
    fragile beauty could be linked
    with such defilement.

Even reason says the branches
    are not strong enough
    to buttress the man's death-wish.

I much prefer to trace the delicacy
    of limb and shaded flower,
    and know, so deep within,
    that force, so rich and real, -
    fair beauty's melancholy ache!

Mourning Wears Many Faces

Mourning wears many faces
       and visits me daily...
It sits on the heart,
       as a mountain boulder delicately balanced,
       poised, ready to tumble and crush
       at the slightest remembering.
It swells, as a sea-side pool, to fullness,
       then ebbs away, only to fill anew
       in ache, and pain, and promise un-fulfilled.
It rests, feather-soft, always there,
       dancing in the air, but just beyond
       the claiming grasp of present knowing.
It hangs heavy on the shoulder...
       a draping weight, pulling one's whole being
       down, down, down, - depression deep.
It reaches out and snags me unexpectedly,
       even when it's been long-stored-away
       for many months or years.
Such loss belongs to timelessness,
       an everyday companion stretching toward eternity
       wearing another mask or face,
       depriving me of joy.

Chalice

       Heralded by jonquil's fanfare
              carried on the stirring breeze,
       Echoed by the dog-tooth violets
              from their home beneath the trees.
       Lilacs heard and held a meeting,
              then withdrew among their leaves.
       Valley lilies pealed a warning
              shyly coiled within their sheaves.
       "Storm is coming!" shouted robins,
              "Better hurry; cover up!"
       But the fearless little tulip
              bravely raised her chalice cup.

Deception

Where does the REAL leave off,
  reflection sharp begin?
Surely the shore breaks clear!
   So clean the demarcation line.

And does the wall protect,
  grant surety secure. . .
Stone-on-stone-on-stone-on-stone?

How deceptive in the seeming!

Southward Flight

On the breast of the pond
    they rested and fed -
    plunging hungrily,
        seeking,
            drawing deep
            the nourishing draughts.

Each moved gracefully
    in ritual choreography -
    stretches, and lifts, and artful preening
        patiently practiced, -
            even a few false starts -
            testing strength.

Then, as one, they rose,
    circled the nurturing space
        in final, grateful salute,
    and raucously urging each other on,
        set the flight formation
            heading south.

Anawim

These corn stocks were caught by early snow,
  the ripe, full ears still hang
  ready for the harvesting,
  waiting, waiting...
  waiting for the picker's tug.

So are the remnant people,
  those known as Anawim,---
  the poor, the trusting faithful few,
  waiting, waiting...
  Awaiting the Messiah's touch!

Sisters Forever

Bonding came early
    while faces were fresh,
    radiant, unlined, expectant...
Brothers they had married
    drew them together;
    family ties were strong.

Seeking support, encouragement, ---
    a friendship shaped itself
    into companioning, - inseparable,
    immutable ties of joys and sorrows shared.

Decades of life's wending ways and journeys
    have etched look-alike lines and smiles;
    each countenance bears the gentle kiss
    of the other's peace and inner strength, -
    loving sisters forever.

Shaping Up

God sometimes "parts my hair" anew -
    forcing a radical move
    from side to side or center.
    It always happens suddenly,
    with an energy and swift surprise,
    I've come to recognize
    as His way with me!

But recently, I've caught Him sculpting me
    with soft styling brush, and fine-tooth comb,
    carefully shaping, as wind has kissed
    and waved and permed this sand,

I've wondered what it's all about,
    and how I'll look when all turned out,
    shaped up and squeaky clean?

Separation

Separation ---

the chasm which is

bridged only by LOVE.

On Seeing A Cardinal In Winter

As fire, flung from Pentecostal breast
    across the shimmering crystal
    surface of the snow,
Your swift flight take...
Your wing, - a strong, a soaring surety;
Your call, - a vibrant summons to my soul.

And then,
    upon the veiled twilight drapes
    which have been cast as shadowed mists
    upon some frosted branch,
Your portrait pause to paint
With calm - the endless "moment-ness" of love,
At peace - adoration's hush, deliberate repose.

Arabesque In D

I would have her make music,
  as she used to do:
  Sonatas and concerti,
  preludes, fugues, and tunes
  to set a toe to tapping.
She knew and played them all,
  then smiled in satisfaction.

But she doesn't know me now!

Today I saw her sitting,
  blank-eyed from medication,
  a table-top before her
  to keep her "poseyed" in.
Her fingers moved in memory
  as some silent melody she played
  upon the table top.

When she had finished with a flourish
  all the chords, the runs and trills,
  she sat back in resignation,
  placing hands into her lap.
I clapped. --- It somehow reached her
  beyond dementia's dreadful veil;
  and looking up, she smiled in recognition.

  Somewhere, somehow...
  her mind directs her fingers
  to caress the magic-music-making keys
  and create a melody sublime.
Though I can not hear it; --- I wish I could,
  and will someday, I'm sure ---
  Yet I have boldly named it,
    "Liz's Arabesque in D."

Command

Sing, Oh thou, my soul!

Sing the joyous canticle
  which burns within your depths ---
  Each word a flame
      enkindled by the showering sparks
      of Love Itself...
      fanned by Living Breath
      unto that
          roaring, soaring
          rumbling, tumbling
      torrent of praise which o'erwhelms
      unto a hushed,--unending
          SILENCE.

Each melody ---
      not separate, disjointed strains
      but one unending flow
      of heart's love -- ceaselessly changing --
      one unto another,
      Yet unbroken, in ever-increasing intensity,
          quickened, heightened, unto a
      breathless repose of adoring
          SILENCE.

      Oh sing, Oh my soul,
              Sing unto Thy God!

Siblings Three

Each one's unique: a special gift
        of Life Himself, molded just so
        by the Creator's Hand,
Then, lent, entrusted, to each other
        and warm parental hearts
        for final fashioning.

The ties are not just arm-holds,
        or embracing, three-way hugs:
More, their stories are entwined;
        their lives irrevocably meshed,
For each has marked the other
        with a sibling's totem sign.

Question

Oh wheat in the wind
    And grape on the vine,
Do you ever dream
    Of your fate divine?

Midnight Rendezvous

I keep a silent rendezvous with pain.
While night pursues its shadowed course, we meet
In calm or passionate embrace, we greet
Until at length, my tortured limbs would fain
Believe, that reason gone, I be not sane.
Perhaps this body's grief, so keen, complete,
Has, as its source, imagination's seat.
Thus mind reflects, as spasm comes again.

But then, the pain is known as something real,
And clasped, held firm as token of Love's seal.
Dawn breaks, upon my face a smile is worn,
Lest by man's prying eyes be shorn,
The virgin joy of hiding all in One,
Who knows, alone, what victories are won.

Virtual Reality

Surround - around...
　　　3D sight and sound...
Light - dark...
　　　Golden - stark...
Silent waft, feeble draft...
　　　Leaf at rest...
　　　On earthen breast...
Truth in One...
　　　And One in Truth.

ALL THINGS SPEAK OF THEE

Cyclical Journey

What a boon to be free,
        to be whole, and real, transformed;
        to have moved into, through, beyond,
        the limitations of the ancient scripted roles,
        Innocent, Orphan, Martyr, Warrior,
        Seeker, Destroyer, Trickster, even Lover.

Each produced its certain fruit,
        its primal terror, intensity, mystery,
        and death-into-life experience.

The Magician's healing touch gave birth:
        transforming, liberating movement,
        personal power, poised visions of what can be,
        and is, in moment, here and now.

The Sage, - the Crone, - awakens as masks, illusions,
        attachments flee in face of ultimate reality -
        a wisdom rich, and wide, and deep,
        with will conformed to Godhead's truth!

Then, the Fool takes over ---
        balancing all by breaking rules,
        innocently acting out all insights, feelings,
        and irreverences... the perfect foil.

Suddenly, it all becomes so clear!
        The Fool, in reaching out to innocence,
        is both the beginning and the end
        of all the inner journeying.

The Watchers

The watchers
Claim their territory:
The bay, the dock, the shore.

They watch and wait ...
For what, for whom?

Perhaps their own Godot?

The Hunger

As hungering birds, endlessly reeling
Through the soul-sky emptiness.
With cadenced cacophony calling, cawing,
mewling,
wailing,
caterwauling,

"Come fill us, Christ, Oh Christ!"

In Streams of Grace

The wind has planted
    snowy kisses
    upon each tangled branch -
    making love with soaring trunk.

My arms would gather
    all into a oneness,
    that my wintery heart
    be warmed -
    washed clean in streams of grace.

Verity

And I have stood tall ---
      at the margin of the world
      seeking the sureness of the
      knowledge just beyond ---
Poised, I have balanced at my
      fingertips the bubble ball
      of faith and life's existence.
Entranced by what was mirrored
      (or was it just pretended?)
      I have drunk deep the sobering
      intoxication of the liquor of the wise.
Only to be crushed, and stupored
      by the swiftness of the leveling
      stroke which leaves me naked ---

'Tis at the heights, one finds
      one's lowest depths.

Swinging at Ninety

I hope to swing at ninety!

...to feel again the joy-filled moment
      of suspense and awe, when chain is taut
      and gravity calls back the arcing weight;

...to know again the gentle shove
      by loving hand to set
      the whole in motion;

...to be again the blonded, pig-tailed child
      with eager eye, fast beating heart,
      who cries out, "Higher! Higher!"

...to fly again, risking all by letting go,
      and tumbling head over heels, over and over
      unto the ever-green grass.

But, IF I swing at ninety ---
      I want to jump, leaping, flying,
      straight out of swinging seat,
      into the arms of GOD

Omega Point

Mystics image mountains moved by faith!

More often they are scaled, crawled,
      clambered without grace or ceremony,
By way of tangled switchbacks,
      sheer rock faces,
         hazardous hairpin turns,
            ledges listing toward infinity,
      ruts, erosion, boulder slides, and fractured timbers.
All forming progress hind'ring barriers
      to the crest's attainment.

How like life's offerings!

Challenging turns and tangles,
      rock-strewn slabs and ledges narrow,
      negotiated painfully with piton, crampon,
         or alpenstock's aid;
      traversed with slow deliberation,
         careful belaying, and pendulous swing,
Defenses learned, employed against the losses,
      the sorrows, and the very stuff of life.

Omega point, the mountain summit, still is sought,
      that I might know the Kiss Divine!

Sunset Serenity

Serenity can't be bidden
        to come into the heart.
Rather...
It steals in, as a sunset colors
        and enflames a western sky.
It moves in, as rippling waters
        are kissed into a lightsome path.
It takes possession, as salt-scented
        seaside air fills waiting lungs.
It makes its presence known
        only by its absent
            present-ness

LOCATION OF SELECTED PHOTOGRAPHS

Absurd Paradox: Kickapoo State Park, Illinois
Anawim: McLean County, Illinois
Arising from the Wreck: Assateague National Seashore, Virginia
Beyond the Veil: Mundelein, Illinois
Blue Mesa Legacy: Door County, Wisconsin
Breakthrough: Turkey Run State Park, Indiana
Command: Cove Point, Door County, Wisconsin
Creation's Dance: Mundelein,Illinois
Deception: Mundelein, Illinois
Doorways Into Doors: Parklands, McLean County, Illinois
Path: St. Marys Church, Champaign, Illinois (Photo by Beth Hand)
God's Sentinels: Parklands, McLean County, Illinois
Golden Path: Mundelein, Illinois
Homestead's Hide and Seek: near Kappa, Illinois
In Streams of Grace: Mackinaw River near Kappa, Illinois
Land of Falling Waters: Kegon Falls, Nikko, Japan
Late Morning Mist: Mundelein, Illinois
Leaning into the Lord: Parklands, McLean County, Illinois
Omega Point: Rocky Mountain National Park, Colorado
Prayer ofthe Troubled Soul: Olympic National Park, Washington
Purposeful Grace: Snowy Egret, Sanibel Island, Florida
Question: Mahomet, Illinois
Quiet Pond: Mundelein, Illinois
Redbuds in Blossom: Mackinaw River near Kappa, Illinois
Ruby Beach: Ruby Beach, Olympic Peninsula, Washington
Separation: Turkey Run State Park, Indiana
Shaping Up: Indiana Dunes National Seashore, Indiana
Solitary Journey: New Glarus Woods, Wisconsin
Southward Flight: Horicon Marsh, Wisconsin
Spring Sunset: Sanibel Island, Florida
Steps into Infinity: Parklands, McLean County, Illinois
"Stumps: Whitefish Point on Lake Superior, Wisconsin
Sunset Serenity: Leighton Point, south of Milbridge, Maine
The Watchers: Chincoteague Island, Virginia
The Yearning: McLean County, Illinois
Untutored Wings: Sanibel Island, Florida
Virgin Territory: Parklands, McLean County, Illinois
Virtual Reality: Mundelein, Ilinois.

RESOURCES

Au, Wilkie; Cannon, Noreen. URGINGS OF THE HEART: A SPIRITUALITY OF INTEGRATION. New York: Paulist Press, 1995.

Barker, Philip. USING METAPHOR IN PSYCHOTHERAPY. New York: Brunner/Mazel, Publishers, 1985.

Bettelheim, Bruno. THE USES OF ENCHANTMENT. New York: Vantage Books, 1977.

Bolen, Jean Shinoda. THE GODDESSES IN EVERY WOMAN: A NEW PSYCHOLOGY OF WOMAN. New York: Harper & Row, 1984.

Borysenko, Joan. FIRE IN THE SOUL: A NEW PSYCHOLOGY OF SPIRITUAL OPTIMISM. New York: Warner Books, 1993.

. . . GUILT IS THE TEACHER, LOVE IS THE LESSON. New York: Warner Books, 1990.

Bradley, Marion Zimmer. THE MISTS OF AVALON. New York: Alfred A. Knopf, 1983.

Bridges, William. TRANSITIONS, MAKING SENSE OF LIFE'S CHANGES. Reading, MA: Addison-Wesley, 1980.

Campbell, Joseph. THE HERO WITH A THOUSAND FACES. Bollingen Series XVII, Princeton, NJ: Princeton University Press, 1949.

. . . THE LOST TEACHINGS OF JOSEPH CAMPBELL. Nine Volumes of Taped Interviews. Redmond, WA: Zygon International, Inc., 1993.

Clift, Jean Dalby. CORE IMAGES OF THE SELF: A SYMBOLIC APPROACH TO HEALING AND WHOLENESS. New York: Crossroads, 1992.

Edinger, Edward F.. EGO AND ARCHETYPE: INDIVIDUATION AND THE RELIGIOUS FUNCTION OF THE PSYCHE. New York: Penguin, 1973.

Eisler, Riane. THE CHALICE AND THE BLADE: OUR HISTORY, OUR FUTURE. San Francisco: Harper & Row, 1987.

Eliade, Mircea. IMAGES AND SYMBOLS: STUDIES IN RELIGIOUS SYMBOLISM. London: Harwill, 1961; Princeton, N.J.: Princeton University Press, 1991.

Harnan, Nicholas, MSC. THE HEART'S JOURNEY HOME: A QUEST FOR WISDOM. Notre Dame, IN: Ave Maria Press, 1992.

Hillman, James. RE-VISIONING PSYCHOLOGY. New York: Harper Collophon Books, 1975.

Houston, Jean. THE SEARCH FOR THE BELOVED: JOURNEYS IN SACRED PSYCHOLOGY. Los Angeles: Jeremy P. Tarcher, 1987.

Jung, Carl G.. MAN AND HIS SYMBOLS. New York: Dell, 1968.

Jung, Emma. ANUMUS AND ANIMA. Dallas: Spring, 1957.

Kelly, Thomas R. A TESTAMENT OF DEVOTION. New York: Harper Brothers, 1941.

L'Engle, Madeleine. WALKING ON WATER: REFLECTIONS ON FAITH AND ART. Wheaton, IL: Harold Shaw Publications, 1980.

Levine, Stephen. HEALING INTO LIFE AND DEATH. New York: Doubleday, 1987.

Madeleva, Sr. Mary, CSC. COLLECTED POEMS. New York: MacMillan, 1947.

Matthews, John. AT THE TABLE OF THE GRAIL: MAGIC AND THE USE OF IMAGINATION. New York: Rutledge & Kegan Paul, 1987.

Madanes, Chloe. STRATEGIC FAMILY THERAPY. San Francisco: Jossey-Bass, 1981.

Maher, John M. Briggs, Dennie, eds. AN OPEN LIFE: JOSEPH CAMPBELL IN CONVERSATION WITH MICHAEL TOMS. New York: Harper & Row, 1989.

May, Rollo. THE CRY FOR MYTH. New York: W. W. Norton & Co., 1991.

Moore, Robert; Gillette, Douglas. KING, WARRIOR, MAGICIAN, LOVER: RE-DISCOVERING THE ARCHETYPE OF THE MATURE MASCULINE. San Francisco: HarperCollins, 1990.

Norman, Dorothy. THE HERO: MYTH/IMAGE/SYMBOL. New York: New American Library, 1969.

Pearson, Carol S.. AWAKENING THE HEROES WITHIN: TWELVE ARCHETYPES TO HELP US FIND OURSELVES AND TRANSFORM OUR WORLD. San Francisco: Harper San Francisco, 1991.

. . . THE HERO WITHIN: SIX ARCHETYPES WE LIVE BY. San Francisco: Harper & Row, 1986.

Rupp, Joyce. DEAR HEART, COME HOME: A PATH OF MIDLIFE SPIRITUALITY. New York: Crossroads, 1996.

. . .MAY I HAVE THIS DANCE. Notre Dame, IN: Ave Maria Press, 1992.

Satir, Virginia. PEOPLE MAKING. Palo Alto: Science and Behavior Books, 1972.

Siegfried, Regina; Morneau, Robert, eds. SELECTED POETRY OF JESSICA POWERS. Kansas City: Sheed and Ward, 1989.

Sofield, Loughlan; Juliano, Carroll; Hammett, Rosine. DESIGN FOR WHOLENESS: DEALING WITH ANGER, LEARNING TO FORGIVE, AND BUILDING SELF-ESTEEM. Notre Dame, IN: Ave Maria Press, 1990.

Teilhard de Chardain, Pierre. THE DIVINE MILIEU. New York: Harper & Row, 1957.

Thompson, Helen, BVM. JOURNEY TOWARD WHOLENESS: A JUNGIAN MODEL OF ADULT SPIRITUAL GROWTH. New York: Paulist Press, 1982.

Turbayne, C. M.. THE MYTH OF THE METAPHOR. Columbia, SC: University of South Carolina Press, 1970.

Ulanov, Ann & Barry. PRIMARY SPEECH: A PSYCHOLOGY OF PRAYER. Atlanta: John Knox Press, 1982.

Walker, Barbara. THE CRONE: WISDOM, AGE, POWER. New York: Harper & Row, 1985.

Wiederkehr, Macrina. SEASONS OF YOUR HEART. San Francisco: HarperSanFrancisco, 1991.